FOREWORD

I am particularly delighted to have been asked to write this foreword for two reasons. First, at the National Maritime Museum Cornwall it is our business to tell stories of the sea, many of which have now been forgotten. One such story is that of the Berwick Smacks. These sloop-rigged vessels built on the banks of the Tweed were the fastest cargo vessels afloat in the late 18th and early 19th centuries, capable of reaching London in less than two days, a speed that could not be matched until the coming of the railways. With their cargoes of fish, grain and passengers these vessels made an enormous contribution to the prosperity of the town. In this book, Jim Walker explains not only the economic background to the emergence of the smacks but also describes life on board and argues that the form of these unique vessels would go on to influence the design of at least one other famous sailing ship, the *Cutty Sark*.

Secondly, I have known Jim Walker for 35 years and indeed in a former role I had the good fortune to collaborate with him on a number of projects, from an exhibition on Thomas Sword Good to his documentary project, *"A Wake for the Salmon"*, in which he recorded the final year of commercial fishing on the lower reaches of the Tweed. I am immensely pleased that Jim is continuing to explore, explain and champion the maritime history of this unique and beautiful town.

Richard Doughty
Director, National Maritime Museum Cornwall

ACKNOWLEDGEMENTS

For the production of this, my tenth book on Berwick,
I have been greatly indebted to the following for the help given.

Richard Doughty

Edinburgh City Arts Centre

National Maritime Museum, Greenwich

Mariners' Museum, London

National Galleries of Scotland

Museum of London

Sheila and Harry Scott

BERWICK SMACKS

"He that begenneth to write a story for the fyrste must with his understanding gather the matter together, set hys words in order and dylygentlye seke out on every part" - LELAND*

Not wishing to seem boastful, but I have been "gathering the matter" together for sixty years, in respect of two aspects of Berwick – its history and its photographic records. But one aspect of Berwick's history, largely unwritten, is its maritime history – in particular the invention and importance of the Berwick Smack, which was conceived, lived and died before the invention of photography. So, what was a Berwick Smack?

The short answer is that it was a fast sailing ship employed in transporting goods and people, but before we delve into the history of the Berwick Smack, let us focus on the foundation and importance of Berwick as a port.

The Author

---

* John Leland was an English antiquary, born in London, travelled much on the Continent, and amassed vast learning; held a commission from Henry VIII to examine the antiquities and libraries of England, in fulfilment of which charge he spent six years in making a collection of records that would otherwise be lost and did so for the rest of his life, till he went insane in arranging them. (1506-1552)

THE PORT OF BERWICK AND FAST SAILING SHIPS

There were two periods when Berwick-on-Tweed enjoyed great prosperity as a port. The first was when it was a Scottish Royal Burgh, and later when it had been an English town for three hundred years.

There is a reference to Berwick as a port as far back as the 9th century, and one story of these early days concerns a citizen of Berwick by the name of Cnut the Opulent. One of his ships had been taken by pirates and Cnut hired and equipped no less than 14 ships from Berwick to give chase. Not only had the pirates taken Cnut's ship, but inadvertently they had also taken Mrs. Cnut, who had been returning from a pilgrimage aboard her husband's ship!

In the 12th Century, King William the Lion of Scotland wanted military assistance from the Counts of Flanders, and he ordered his emissaries to go to Berwick *"where they will find the boatmen who will take them to Flanders, - they will sail direct for Flanders and not sail down the coast of England"*. It follows from this that the Berwick boatmen were skilled in navigation, and indeed trade between Berwick and the Low Countries was already well established.

By the 13th century, Berwick was Scotland's largest and most prosperous burgh, due to its port. Perhaps 15% of its population would be speaking a foreign tongue, principally Flemish, but also German.

The Red Hall was where the Flemings had their headquarters cum factory, while the German traders occupied the White Hall.

In 1286 Berwick reached its maritime peak when £2,190 was paid to the Scottish Exchequer, in respect of customs duty. It does not seem much now, but this sum was equal to a quarter of the total customs for the whole of England. This was when Berwick was described as a second Alexandria, such was its prosperity.

The main export was wool, but hides, salmon, and other fish were also exported in large quantities. The wool and hides were gathered from the Tweed Basin under the jurisdiction of the great monasteries of Melrose, Kelso, Jedburgh and Dryburgh, and no fewer than 15 religious orders had large properties and warehouses in Berwick to handle this commerce.

One of these religious orders, the Augustinians, had a hospital at Soutra, near Edinburgh, with a warehouse in

Berwick. Following excavations at Soutra in the 1980's by Dr Brian Moffat, it has come to light that, among other imports, Mediterranean sponges were shipped into Berwick for use in the hospital. Before being shipped, the sponges were soaked in a solution of opium poppy, hemlock and henbane and then dried. Once received at Soutra, the sponges were re-activated by water and were used as an anaesthetic during operations on patients.

A major import was wine – the monasteries required it for their religious ceremonies, armies marched on it and royal households must have bathed in it by the quantities ordered. In 1253, 400 hogsheads of wine were sent to Alexander III's court (Alexander was 12 years of age!) and this was equivalent to more than 250,000 bottles. Later in Alexander's reign he had to pledge all the duties paid in the Port of Berwick for a whole year to cover one outstanding wine bill. Even after Alexander's death, his successor John De Baliol had to answer for his forebear's debt to a Bordeaux wine merchant by the name of Jean Mazun (or John Mason). Poor Mr Mason died some years later – his debt still unpaid.

Most of the wine trade from Bordeaux and the Low Countries (Rhenish) came through Berwick, and even after Edward I of England sacked Berwick in 1296, huge supplies of wine for his armies campaigning in Scotland were shipped into Berwick.

Berwick's commercial maritime trade now began its decline, due to its increasing military importance as an English bridgehead. During Edward I's campaigns against the Scots he summoned a huge assemblage of 81 ships to Berwick in the years 1301 to 1303. Thereafter for almost two centuries Berwick was the cockpit for Scotland and England's struggles. After 1482, when Berwick was finally an English possession, having changed hands probably 17 times, the rich hinterland of the Tweed valley was effectively cut off. It was not until the Union of Parliaments in 1707 that things began to look up once more for Berwick as a major maritime centre.

In 1751 a gentleman named Arthur Byram was sufficiently attracted to Berwick, that he started a shipbuilding business, and this lasted for well over a century. Byram's principal claim to fame must be as the originator of a new type of ship which became known as the Berwick Smack.

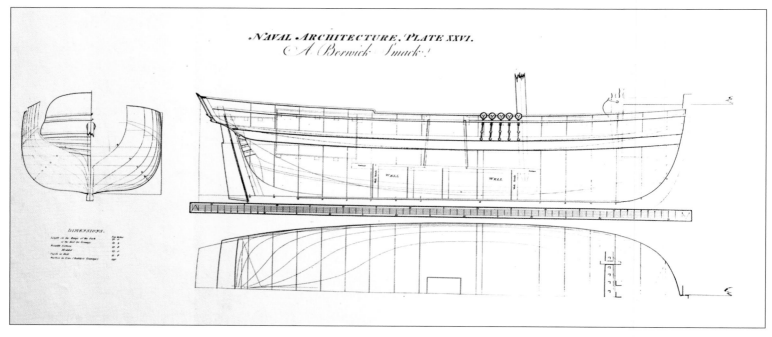

The original of this plan, clearly labelled a Berwick Smack is in the Science Museum in London and dates from 1804.

Prior to the appearance of the Berwick Smack, Tweed salmon had been conveyed in large quantities to London by small trading vessels from the Thames. Most of the salmon, at that time, was salted and packed in barrels.

The introduction of the Berwick Smack, however, enabled the Berwick freemen coopers to take over the shipping trade, for the smacks provided a fast, safe and reliable delivery to London. After 1788, ice was being used which allowed Tweed salmon to be sold fresh in London within a few days of being caught.

The Berwick Smacks' reputation for efficiency and fast passage attracted goods and passengers, so that by 1806 there were 62 carriers coming into Berwick, not only from Tweeddale, but also from Carlisle, Dumfries, Edinburgh, and Glasgow.

The transport by land of heavy goods between Edinburgh and Berwick, for onward shipping to London, was greatly facilitated by the building of Pease Bridge in 1786. This bridge was the highest bridge in the world at the time of building. The bridge (approximately 1 mile south east from Cockburnspath - 16 miles from Berwick) allowed heavy wagons, pulled by teams of horses, to cross the hitherto impassable steep ravine.

Among the passengers of the smacks was Sir Walter Scott, who was a frequent traveller and indeed one smack bore his name.

He wrote that, *"the mail coach and Berwick Smacks have done more than the Union (i.e. Scotland and England 1707) in altering our national character, sometimes for the better and sometimes for the worse."**

Confirming Scott's view was an item in Chambers 'Picture of Scotland', published in 1828, which states that the women of Berwick are without the exception of even Edinburgh or Inverness, the most beautiful to be found north of the Tweed – *"they possess the utmost elegance of form and dress with taste equal to their native graces, on account it is said, of the facility with which they procure the fashions from London, by means of the Smacks."*

Having established the benefits of this remarkable ship we should look at the actual vessel itself and we find that the earliest smacks were about 100 tons burthen**, but over the years increased to 200 tons or more, allowing a greater degree of comfort for passengers, while not sacrificing the speed which was essential for the fast conveyance of fresh salmon to the London Market. Not only was salmon, grain and of course passengers shipped to London, but also large quantities of eggs, which were used in the refining of sugar.

Eggs were gathered from all over the Borders by "egglers" who then transported them to Berwick by leading panier equipped horses along the rough roads.

---

*   Source Lockhart 448-450 Scott writing from Ashiestiel 7/4/1806
** Burthen: The tonnage of a ship based on the number of tuns of wine it could carry in its holds

This delightful scene, captured by an unknown artist at the beginning of the 19th century, shows a smack beached on the foreshore with two horses and carts waiting for cargo to be unloaded. Tweedmouth in the distance shows a tall chimney emitting smoke adjacent to a substantial building. Good's directory of 1806 describes such a building as a Steam Mill – "the first thing of its kind". Several salmon fishing crews ply their nets, and at least three brigs or smacks hug Berwick's quay.

Return voyages from London brought a multitude of goods including large quantities of London beer and porter which would be distributed by the extensive network of carriers operating out of Berwick. And of course we must not forget the latest fashions, which 'Chambers Picture of Scotland' mentions.

The Berwick Smack was rather blunt bowed with a broad beam, but with a huge spread of sail and one very strong centrally placed mast. This allowed them to sail *"nearer the wind"* and maintain a fast speed, even under adverse conditions.

A crew of 11 were required to manage the huge amount of sail deployed. They could sail at between 9 and 11 knots per hour and a fast voyage to London from Berwick could be done in 44 hours, but depending on current and wind could take 5 days or even longer.

Further the doughty sea-farer was allowed more luggage at no extra cost and as regards the discomfort of sea-sickness, John Reid, Bookseller in Bridge Street, Berwick, sold anti-bilious pills, also guides for smack passengers describing what they would see on the voyage.

This fine half model of a Berwick Smack was crafted by John Cowe B.Sc., who is a marine draughtsman and was a shipyard manager with a life long interest in Berwick Smacks.

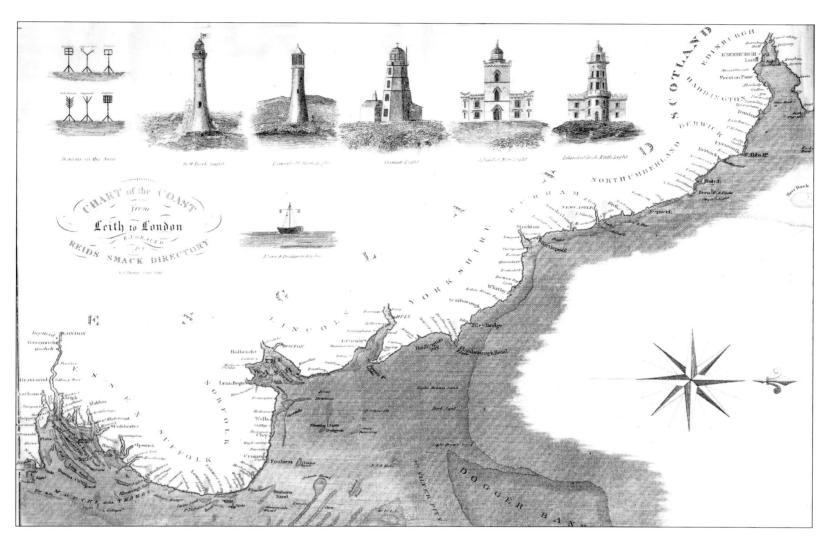

A fold-out map of the coast from Leith to London, contained in Reid's Smack Directory, which prospective smack passengers could purchase. This directory had spaces to record their voyage and was illustrated with helpful maps and details of what could be seen on their journey.

In the guides Spittal is noted thus, *"The Village that stands upon the southern bank of the Tweed, at its very mouth, is Spittle. This is almost wholly inhabited by sea-fairing people, who not infrequently, convey in their boats, tourists and parties of pleasure to Holy Island."*

"They used to be reckoned of peculiarly unaccommodating dispositions and boisterous manners!"

Another book published in 1815 was titled, 'A trip to London or the Humours of a Berwick Smack'. This was a factual account of an actual voyage, but with humorous overtones. The voyage began on Friday 13th May, 1813. The captain was Captain Taylor from Berwick *("who answered every interrogation with great politeness")*, and the smack was named Tweed (built by Bruce in 1792).

The cook on this voyage – for all meals were included in the fare – *"had only one arm and was an unusually black and a grim figure. On the wooden stump of one arm, he supported a bucketful of water, while the only hand he possessed, clenched fast a large piece of beef he was about to wash. He was indeed the personification of dirtiness."*

Nevertheless, the author describes the meals as being excellent, so it must have been a smooth trouble-free voyage.

Two years later the passengers of the *Tweed* Packet (or Smack) were not so fortunate in January 1815, when they encountered extremely stormy weather all along the east coast, the voyage taking five days, instead of the more normal two to two and a half days.

The passengers were so grateful, they presented the Captain (James Findley aged 29*), with a token of respect in the shape of an engraved silver snuff box, with *"thanks for his superior seamanship and perseverance under the most serious difficulties from the state of the weather."*

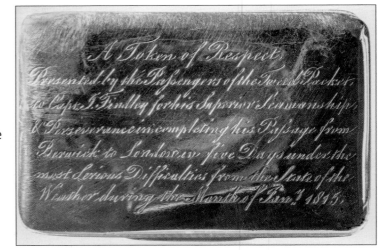
Silver snuffbox presented to Captain J Findlay by his grateful passengers.

---

* Captain Findley was a resident of Tweedmouth. He died in 1833 aged 47 and is buried in Tweedmouth Parish Churchyard. Regarded as an intrepid seaman, his last command was the Stately.

This painting by Thomas Sword Good c. 1831 is entitled 'The F'cstle of a Berwick Smack'.
It shows the cramped conditions the crews had to endure, and how they had to share the space with equipment and dripping wet hawsers.

When stormy weather threatened, all hands had to turn out and take down the mainsail quickly. Three taps on the top of the forecastle hatch by the ship's mate, was the signal for urgent action by all the crew. In the dark, with blinding rain or snow, it was a dangerous operation, and lives were lost.

One survivor of these hazardous days was a Samuel Gradon who died in 1917 aged 94. Samuel served his apprenticeship on the Berwick Smack, *King William*, starting as a Cabin Boy, and rising to Skipper within the Berwick Shipping Company's fleet. His was a hard life, but he would be respected for his skill as a Captain both by the crew and also the many distinguished guests he transported safely between Berwick and London.

As already stated, Sir Walter Scott was a frequent passenger, likewise David Hume, the eminent Scottish philosopher who resided at Ninewells, Chirnside. Hume stated that *"Everything in the world is purchased by labour"* and it would be nice to think that he would be appreciative of the work of the crews of the smacks, catering for his safety and comfort*.

A ludicrous and rather cruel cartoon supposedly showing the dining area and sleeping bunks of a smack in bad weather.

It is unlikely that the Duke of Roxburgh or Lord Bredalbane would philosophise about the crew when they were passengers on the smacks. Likewise, Mr. William Cobbett (1763-1835) famous for his book, *'Tour in Scotland'* in which he berates the Lord Chancellor, Brougham, *"for being a very desperate Edinburgh Reviewer just arrived in London in a Berwick Smack, freighted to the very choking of the hold with adventurers, come to get pickings out of the loons o' the Sooth**. You have carried on your botheration pretty well (since then)."*

A more charitable passenger using the Berwick smacks was one John Scott, who worked in the Carron Warehouse in London. Originating from the Scottish Borders, John wrote regularly to his cousin John Walker, who had a thriving merchant's business in Selkirk.

On the 26th October 1793, John Scott (concerned about his cousin's health) wrote, *"If you still continue poorly, you cannot do better than come up here (London) as the voyage will certainly be of great service to you."*

---

* While in London (February 1739) Hume wished for a passage back home, but "contrary winds have kept all Berwick ships from sailing" – a passage became available sometime after.

** Menial scamps

The Pool of London by Thomas Luny (1759-1837) showing smacks with St. Pauls Cathedral in the background c.1800

John Scott had arrived in London on the 19th September, 1793, after a five day voyage from Berwick (a long voyage, perhaps due to a dearth of favourable winds). This was however, quicker than his friend's journey, Mr. Smith, who had opted to travel to London by stagecoach, and whose journey took two days longer.

John Scott goes on, *"My fellow passengers were all very agreeable and only eleven, which made it more so, as we were not overcrowded."*

John goes on to write, *"I was as sick in coming up as in going down, would make but a bad sailor."* However, romance is in the air for he asks his cousin to *"Please make my kind respects to Miss Dalziel. Tell her I expect she will accompany you, and if she likes London better than Earlston she shall be welcome to stay than go back, and tell John and Mary that they shall come up and see their Aunt. I hope the young Lady is doing very well."*

Miss Dalziel's father was a minister of religion in Earlston and his name crops up regularly in purchases made from John Walker (General Dealer in Selkirk), whose day book records all the sales.

In 1790, sugar and herring were supplied. There were repeated purchases of cheese (10 to 11 lbs weight), tea, brandy, wine, rum, canvas, velveteen material, buttons, boot hose (stockings?) and on February 28th 1794, a final item was for black lead. The last item would be for the servants to black-lead the grates in the manse.

It would appear that the Revd Dalziel and his family enjoyed a very comfortable lifestyle and that John Scott aspired to become a member of that family.

In January 1794, Scott, concerned for his cousin's health, arranges for a barrel of fine mild porter to be shipped to Mr James Graham*, Merchant, Berwick, for onward transmission to Walker. The porter was shipped at the Red Lion Wharf, Thames Street, London, aboard the smack Tweed, under the command of Captain Ord. The porter was to be tapped, as soon as it arrived, bottled and well corked, and then laid down in sawdust for a few weeks.

In Walker's records are details of an order fulfilled by a firm of nurserymen, John Callender, of Newcastle. Various types of grass seed, packed in sacks, were shipped on the smack *Neptune* under Captain Ord, sailing from Newcastle on its voyage to Berwick (April 1792). Likewise, the smack *Betsy* carried a consignment of lintseed to Walker. These smacks were listed as Newcastle traders and formed part of the efficient system operated by the shipping companies of Berwick.

---

* Mr James Graham was acting as a forwarding agent. Graham had premises on the east side of the Marygate (High St) and is listed in Good's 1806 directory as a Twine Spinner and Starch Maker and probably had premises at the Starch House Toll, Mordington.

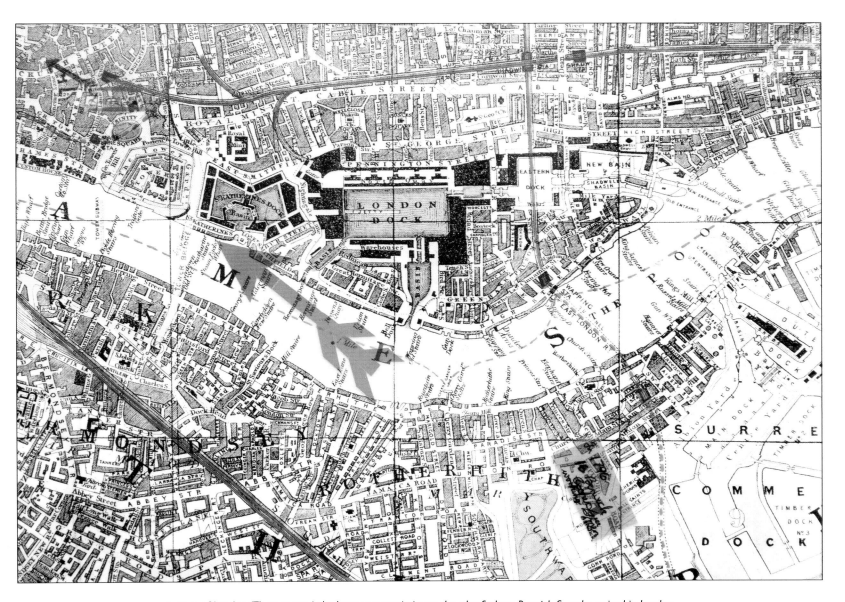

A Map of London (Thames area) the large arrow pointing to the wharf where Berwick Smacks arrived in London.

The greatest number of smacks sailing from Berwick was 21 in 1799, roughly half belonging to the Old Shipping company, and the others to the Union Shipping Company.

In 1806 the Old Shipping Company, which was formed by coopers prior to 1766, had twelve smacks:-

King George	Caledonia	London
Queen Charlotte	Brittania	Neptune
Swallow	Berwick Merchants	Albion
Commercial	London and Berwick	Tweed – captained by Jeremiah Ward

The Union Shipping Company, founded in 1798 as competitors to the Old Shipping Co. had 8 smacks. They were: -

Edinburgh	Leith
Fifeshire	Glasgow
Eliza	Roxburgh
Sprightly	Coldstream

The trade for both these Berwick companies increased rapidly, with carriers' carts and wagons from Glasgow and the West coming in every day.

Business boomed, but thinking to get an even bigger share of passengers and goods, they began to start some of their smacks from Leith (the port for Edinburgh). This proved to be a bad move, for a group of Leith merchants, observing this profitable trade, set up the Edinburgh and Leith Shipping Company in 1802 and had six Berwick Smacks built, but not at Berwick, but at Bridport in Devon, a centre for sailing ship construction.

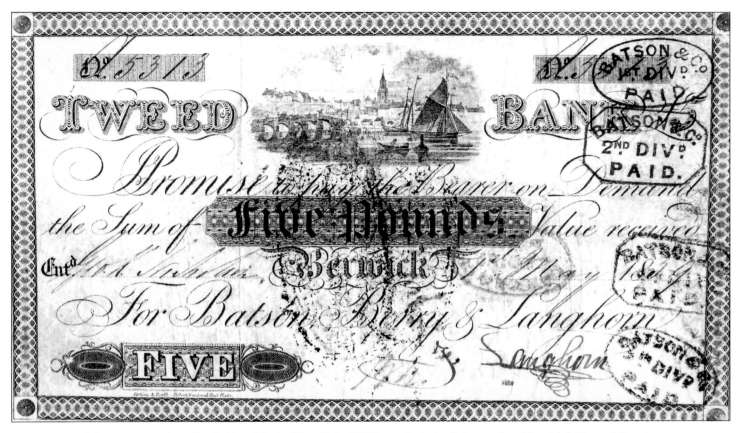

A five pound note, issued by the Tweed Bank of Berwick in 1839, has a finely detailed engraving of Berwick Bridge and Quayside showing a Berwick Smack in full sail. The Tweed Bank failed in 1841, and holders of these notes had to present them to the bank, at designated intervals, to receive part payments.

Another company was formed in 1809, The London and Edinburgh Shipping Company, and they took over six smacks from the Berwick Union Company, and had five more built by the shipbuilding firm of William Good of Bridport.

Acquisitions and closures were hazards to be overcome, but an ever pressing problem was the fear of loss by enemy action. The Napoleonic wars (1803 -1815) coupled with press gangs and privateers made for a period when the safety of ships, cargoes, crews and passengers could not be taken for granted.

In 1807, George Cleghorn* of Rulewater, voyaged to London on one of the best appointed smacks, and within a few hours of sailing, a British man of war was observed sending off a crewed boat which made directly for the smack.

The captain of the smack, who had been watching carefully with his telescope, concluded they were about to be press-ganged. This was a practice adopted by the British Navy, who made raids on land or sea for the purpose of obtaining men to augment depleted ships' crews. This practice resulted in men being uprooted from their families and work, and being kept at sea for years without any means of redress.

The captain of the smack ordered the able-bodied men of the crew to hide themselves in the cargo, which left only a few old men and boys to represent the crew. When interrogated by the Naval Lieutenant, the captain swore that they had already been press-ganged earlier in the voyage, and he was having to use his passengers as crew.

The passengers were lined up for inspection by the Naval Officer, who, while not convinced, left the smack with a warning that the next time he came across the captain of the smack *"he would take all on board"*.

As soon as it was safe to do so, the captain of the smack had the crew hoist *"every bit of canvas there was"*. With a good breeze and every sail billowing the smack made its escape, despite being fired on by the Navy, who by this time realised they had been duped.

The passengers would no doubt think their troubles were over, but as the smack continued its journey and was sailing off the Yorkshire coast a 'strange sail' was seen some distance on the left. The skipper of the smack did not like her appearance, so he made preparations for defence, loading his small three-pound shot cannons while preparing to make a run for it. The wind, now favouring the smack, allowed her to leave behind the French privateer** (as it proved to be). The able-bodied passengers, no doubt to their relief, were then able to return the pistols and cutlasses to the smacks' armoury, these weapons having been issued to them at the commencement of the alarm.

A year later, Captain Nesbitt, master of the smack *Queen Charlotte*, returned fire on a cutter privateer of 16 guns. This action took place off Newbiggin on the Northumberland coast, and in a strange vagary of the Napoleonic Wars, the privateer was formerly named the *Argus* – a British Government's Excise ship, which had been previously captured by the French.

---

* Proprietor of the Weens Estate in Rulewater near Hawick. In 1773 the old house at Weens was pulled down and a new mansion was built, with the best imported Baltic timber, brought from the port of Berwick on Tweed by wagons.

** Privateer – A ship which had a licence from its Government to seize enemy ships. This was during the Napoleonic Wars.

Port of Leith circa 1824 by Alexander Nasmyth, showing smacks and Arthur's Seat in the background

Also joining in the broadsides against the privateer was Captain Nesbit of the smack *Caledonia*, who was a son of the captain of the *Queen Charlotte*. The privateer's sails and rigging were shattered and she retired from the fray. Several of the crew of the smacks received musket shot wounds, but none were fatal.

We have previously quoted from a book published in 1815 – *'The Humours of a Berwick Smack'*. This book, while written in a light-hearted fashion, shows a darker side when referring to a certain Smack Captain only by his initials. The initials J.W. stand for Jeremiah Ward (latterly, the Captain of the *Tweed* smack) who died in 1808.

His tombstone in Berwick Parish Churchyard (now lost) described him as *"an honest man and famous seaman"*. So he was, but he was also thought by many, to have sold his soul to the Devil for *"advantages of wind and currents"* – two attributes essential for a sailing ship renowned for fast passages.

His pact with the Devil was supposed to have been signed when his smack was sailing past Scarborough Castle. The incident was recorded thus –

"Most unusually, J.W. was well behind the other smacks sailing north. Not a little put out at this, and storming and swearing greatly, he ordered all crew to go below, and close the hatches so no one could see.

Then, there was a shrill and supernatural whistling, and when in a short time J.W. summoned all hands on deck, they saw that instead of being well behind, they were now leading the other vessels."

The idea that Ward could conjure up wind may have some truth in it, for, in his papers, written in his own hand, is a *"Remedy for a pain of the breast, the back or the side."*

Succinctly, he has written *"Put as much gunpowder and loaf sugar as will lay on a shilling. Take it five mornings at fasting in a glass of gin and whisky."*

While the alcohol might well result in a cheerier outlook, the gunpowder is a different matter, for it comprises saltpetre, sulphur and carbon. Saltpetre is a diuretic, sulphur acts as a laxative, and carbon (like charcoal biscuits) is used to expel wind.

It might be surmised therefore any person ingesting such a mixture, would require no assistance from the Devil in conjuring up wind!

That smacks were well-armed in the tumultuous times of the French Wars is confirmed by James Good's Directory of 1806 in which it is stated *"they are well-found and manned – they carry six or eight carronades bored for 18 lb shot and ammunition of all kinds"*

On the Quay at Leith, c.1825, by D.O. Hill, shows a busy scene, with smacks being loaded and unloaded.

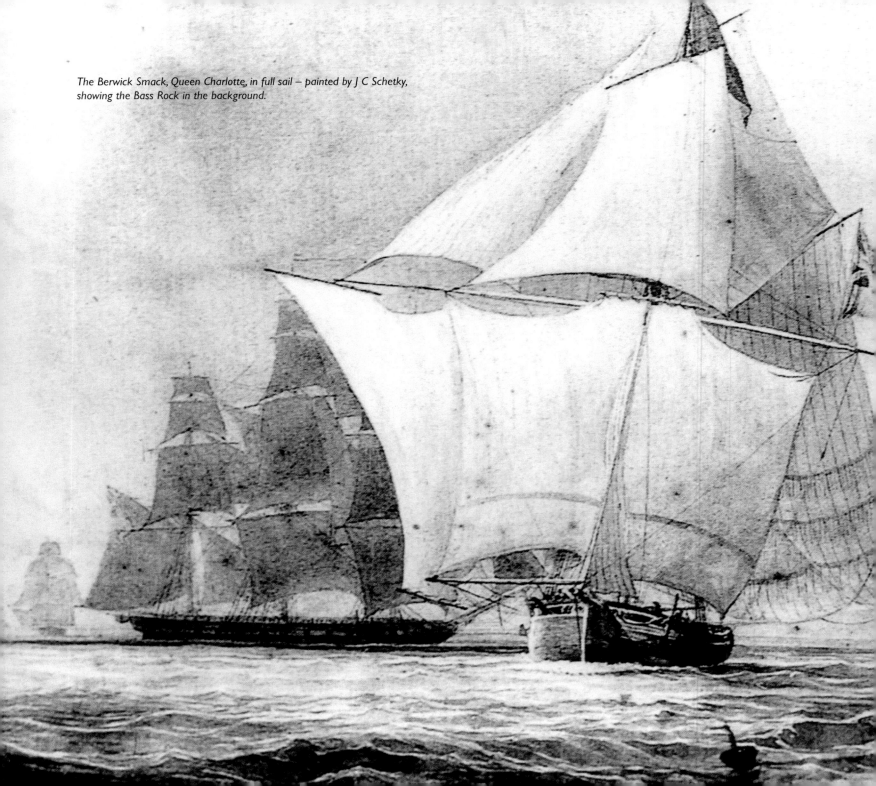

The Berwick Smack, Queen Charlotte, in full sail – painted by J C Schetky, showing the Bass Rock in the background.

No doubt our previously mentioned smack passenger, John Scott, would be well acquainted with the armaments of the smacks, for his employer in London, the Carron Company, supplied the carronades and shot. In the Carron warehouse, where John worked, would be a huge range of wrought iron goods from stoves to spinning machines, balustrades to bedsteads and grates to guns.

It's no wonder, therefore, that the Carron Company of Falkirk required a wharf, named the Carron Wharf, (near the Tower of London), also huge warehouses to handle consignments of their goods brought by sea to London from Falkirk.

Carronades caught the public's attention but more importantly the Admiralty's attention, so that at the Battle of Trafalgar, Nelson's ship the *Victory*, had two 68 pounders, as well as carronades of lesser bore throughout the fleet.

The publicity regarding these guns would rebound favourably on the Berwick Shipping Company's fortunes, for would-be passengers could be reassured of their safety.

Notwithstanding this, our previously mentioned smack passenger Lord Breadalbane, requested a six pounder carronade to fire from his shoulder. Wisely the Carron Company turned down this "suicidal request".

Returning to John Scott, whose romantic hopes were pinned on Miss Dalziel of Earlston – he writes in 1794 of starting a business in London, retailing carpets which he would get from an established carpet manufactory, Robinsons in Hawick (Roxburghshire). The carpets would be shipped by smack from Berwick to London and Miss Dalziel would manage his carpet warehouse.

Alas, Robinsons had ceased to trade by 1810, and sadly Miss Dalziel seems to have died a spinster, being buried in Earlston church cemetery under her own name.

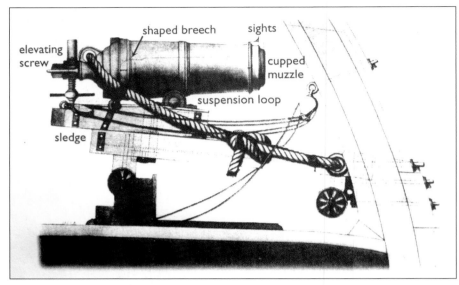

Carronade – invented and made by the Carron Co. Falkirk and used extensively for defence by the Berwick Smacks.

Documents in the author's possession show consignments of goods in smacks from London and Newcastle.

From London, a firm of seedsmen at No 63 The Strand (Messrs Minier, Minier & Co) sent by smack:-

10 lbs of Larch Fir	3 cwt of fine Red Clover contained in 2 strong sacks
12 lbs of Scotch Fir	2 canvas bags
4 lbs of Silver Fir	

All per Captain Nesbitt of Berwick (captain of the *Lively*).

A more unusual cargo from London to Berwick was recorded on 5th February, 1781, when Captain Amey's wife gave birth to a son while on board a smack named the *Berwick Packet* as it sailed down The Thames.

Four years later, the same ship, under a different skipper (Captain Wait) went aground on the Great Farne Island in a tremendous storm, and although all on board and most of the cargo was saved, the loss of the smack (one of the best in the fleet) resulted in the Old Shipping Co. losing upwards of £1,400, a considerable sum in those days.

Panoramic View c. 1812 of London showing a lighter unloading cannon alongside Tower Crane Wharf adjacent to Carron warehouse.

In stormy conditions, water could enter the passengers' saloons so the bunks where they slept were furnished with shutters to overcome splashing, as the water rolled from side to side.

For passengers who still had an appetite, the plates and dishes on the dining tables were restrained by long thin bags of sand, but the menu was anything but restrained, featuring red herring for breakfast, broth, sirloin for lunch, and for tea a huge bacon ham with numerous dishes of tea.

Smack passengers undoubtedly had to possess fortitude in large measure, and faith in the Captain.

When the Berwick Smacks were at the height of their popularity, Berwick would present a busy, vibrant scene to an onlooker, with iron wheels rattling over the cobles, as the horses pulled their loads to discharge on the quayside.

While the smacks were being loaded, passengers for the voyage would be arriving, some of them no doubt having spent the night in a local inn, perhaps pondering on the perils of the sea voyage ahead and the thought of sea sickness.

Why then were the smacks so popular? As always, it comes down to money; for the cost of a passage to London was about £4, but could be as much as £12 depending on demand. The journey by road was also £12, but the cost of the sea trip included food (if the passengers could face it), whereas victuals on the land journey were extra. Time was another factor as the sea voyager could step ashore in the centre of London two days after embarking at Berwick, whereas the coach took four or five days.

The Stately Berwick Smack owned by the Old Shipping Co of Berwick.
This is an oil painting on boards, which, until recently, hung in a bedroom in the Kings Arms Hotel, Berwick. The Stately was built for the London/Berwick trade, and was one of two Berwick smacks built outwith the town (Montrose) such was the demand for these fast ships.

Leith & Berwick Wharf, Irongate, London.

Another consideration was comfort, for although the earlier smacks were only 100 tons burthen, the later smacks were double this, allowing a degree of comfort unknown to the coach passenger.

Each smack had two cabins, one for ladies and the other for gentlemen, with separate bunks which could be closed off for each passenger. During the day the gentlemen's cabin, which had a large central area, became the eating saloon for all passengers, except the steerage passengers, who ate 'al fresco'. The décor was of a high standard. *"The cabins are painted, highly decorated with brass work and gilding, handsomely furnished, and lighted from above during the day, by an ample skylight, at night by a superb lamp, and even piano fortes have of late been introduced."*

This degree of comfort for the smacks' passengers is in sharp contrast to voyagers in earlier days, when they had to travel on brigs. These vessels were two masted sailing ships, used for the conveyance of goods and passengers, and very uncomfortable they were, with cramped accommodation in one cabin and limited hold capacity.

A page from a sketch book owned by Thomas Sword Good (Berwick's famous artist, 1789-1872), showing a brig on the left and a smack (not to scale) on the right.

Brigs were primarily cargo carrying boats and their biggest trade by far was coal transported from the North East of England to London.

Newcastle was the world's greatest coal exporter and 8000 collier brigs arrived in London annually. If there was a hold-up, and brigs were prevented from discharging in London, there was a coal shortage in the Capital.

It was a hard life for the seamen, but it was said that the very best seamen were trained on the Scottish and North East of England coastal trade ships.

It was a rough trade indeed, for empty coal brigs returning from London, were chartered to bring barrels of urine from the Eastend pubs for use in the Yorkshire alum mining industry. The urine was converted to ammonia crystals for tanning leather and dying wool.

The Prospect of Whitby —
this tavern still surviving, is believed to date
back to 1520 and would be well known to the
crews of the Berwick smacks being situated
in the Wapping area where there was a
flourishing Scottish community.

Berwick was prominent in this coastal trade to London, but it was salmon which was the cargo, not coal, and so the introduction of the fast and commodious smack had transformed the maritime scene. Until this time most of the salmon had been salted and packed in barrels of the 'Berwick bind' by the freemen coopers. But in 1788, for the first time, ice was used to keep the salmon fresh.

So, the combination of fast transport and fresh ice-packed salmon, energised the coastal trade even more.

Panoramic view c. 1812 of London showing Billingsgate market with Berwick Smacks unloading in the recessed wharf (top centre).

In Berwick special ice houses were built, and ice gathered in the winter was stored in these large subterranean caverns for use by the merchants sending fresh salmon to the market of Billingsgate in London. If enough ice had not been obtained, more was brought from Norway by chartered ships.

The ice house on Bank Hill has its entrance under the Tweed Bridge.

Although Byram's Berwick Smack takes pride of place in Berwick's maritime history, other shipbuilding yards were in operation over the river on the Tweedmouth shore, building other types of ship.

In 1806 there were two ship-builders in Berwick – Gowans on the Berwick side and Mr Joseph Todd on the Tweedmouth side.
This pen and ink drawing by the author, is based on a rough sketch by J M Turner, which clearly shows two ships being built on the foreshore at Tweedmouth.

The yard of William Bruce was probably the predecessor of Joseph Todd, who flourished briefly in the early 1800's. Todd's yard was engaged in building warships for the British Navy. *H.M.S. Rover,* one of these warships, was a large man of war of 382 tons and was 100 feet in length and carried 16 x 32 lb carronades and 2 x 6 lb guns. Another warship was *H.M.S. Forward*, which took part in a decisive naval action in 1808 against Danish vessels during the Napoleonic Wars, when 40 Danish ships were burned and 10 captured. Like many another Government contractor though, Todd found working for the Admiralty exacting and unprofitable and he was adjudged bankrupt in 1808.

A sketch, which has been attributed to Turner (doubtful!) shows smacks sailing in an estuary, and a vessel being built on the stocks near the water line. It does illustrate how ships were built at this time, and the foreshore at the Tweedmouth end of the old bridge, was the site for two shipbuilding yards.

Byram on the other hand, and his successors, continued to trade profitably up until 1878, and built some beautiful clipper schooners, which were very successful fast ships, and outdid the Berwick smacks for speed, being able to do the journey to London in 30 hours. These clipper schooners not only worked the London trade but also voyaged to Europe, the Mediterranean and the Baltic.

Clipper Schooner Teviot 133 tons register built by A & B Gowan, Berwick and photographed off Berwick c 1900.
This photograph, restored from a broken lantern slide, provides us with rare evidence of an actual Gowan's ship in its final years.

A story concerning the *Teviot* when it was lying alongside an Aberdeen clipper, both berthed at Archangel. The two ships were bound for London and ready to set sail. The two skippers agreed to race to the Thames – the winning skipper would receive a long hat, and his crew would get a tripe supper at a public house in London known to both crews.

The *Teviot* arrived in London, discharged her cargo of oats, then loaded up for Berwick and was going down the Thames when she espied the Aberdeen ship coming up the river – newly arrived. A decisive win for the Berwick ship!

These clipper schooners with their graceful slim lines were the forerunners of the famous Tea Clipper Ships, and perhaps the most famous of them all the *Cutty Sark*, has a rather unique connection with the port of Berwick. The *Cutty Sark* was built to the order of John Willis Junior in the year 1869. John Willis Senior, his father, born in Eyemouth, 10 miles north of Berwick, ran away to sea when he was 12, after a violent disagreement with his guardian uncle. The young lad had thrown a rock at his overbearing uncle and laid him out. Fearing retribution, he signed on as ship's boy on a coasting vessel, probably at Berwick. He learnt his trade the hard way, for it was always said that the best seamen came from the Scottish and North East of England coastal trade ships.

Wax seal of the Berwick Shipping Company c.1856 showing a clipper schooner as its insignia.

Captains like Findley and Ward were fearsome and fearless and their knowledge of winds, currents and tides was awesome. The young John Willis must have absorbed the knowledge and the confrontational attitude to pain and danger, which was inherent in these larger than life figures, for later in life he exhibited exactly the same qualities.

John Willis, still in his teens, became a seaman on a West Indiaman sailing out of London. When berthed at London after a voyage, his ship was docked in the newly-built West India Docks (1802) and as the docks had been excavated from a marshy area, the surrounds were extremely muddy. A hostelry, the Blue Posts, was a favourite inn for the ship captains, but their boots got very muddy trekking there. Young John spotted an opportunity to make money by offering a boot cleaning service. He accumulated a small sum of money and remembering the West Indian Plantation slaves and their love of banjo playing, he invested in fiddle strings which he subsequently sold on his next voyage making a tidy little profit. On succeeding voyages to the West Indies, John bought and sold other commodities, steadily accumulating his capital.

John's big break came, when, having risen to the position of ship's mate, the West Indiaman he was on went aground in bad weather in the English Channel. The Captain and crew abandoned the ship to save their lives, but Willis remained on board, thus preventing plundering. The bad weather eased, the cargo was saved, and the underwriters in their gratitude gave him a large reward which he invested in a ship of which he was the commander.

Willis prospered, and this was a period when large fortunes could be made by bold acquisitive purchases. He added to his fleet until he owned ten ships. The names of the ships were all local names, for he never forgot his roots, so we have: *Whitadder; Blackadder; Borderer; Merse; Lammermuir; St Abbs; John Willis; Janet Willis,* and last but not least the *Tweed*. Did Willis perhaps serve under the irascible Faustian character Jeremiah Ward on the famous Berwick smack the *Tweed*? It is quite possible for Willis, more than once, left other ships sheltering in the Downs, while he took advantage of wind and current to make a fast passage to Demerara. There, loading up with rum and sugar at a high rate of freight, he sped back taking advantage of the Westerly gales which were still keeping his competitors wind-bound in the Downs. Shades of Jeremiah Ward!

Four of John Willis's sons at one time or another commanded ships belonging to their father. The best known and most successful was the eldest, also called *John*.

In a sea shanty entitled *"Stormalong"* both Father and Son are immortalised – Old Stormy was John Senior, and Old Stormy's Son, and the ship he built, was John junior, the ship being the *Cutty Sark.*

The *Cutty Sark* was intended for the Chinese tea trade, but was built when the trade was declining. Steam ships were being used more and more and when the Suez Canal opened (1869) the clipper ships were at a disadvantage.

However, where the clippers scored was in the long voyages from Australia carrying wool.

The *Cutty Sark* was built to the highest specifications laid down by John Willis Jr., and just as the River Tweed connects the Scottish Borders' Counties of Peeblesshire, Roxburghshire, Selkirkshire, and Berwickshire, so do ships named the *Tweed* connect events in the history of the Willis family. One of the most successful ships that old Willis owned was the *Tweed*. Originally it had been named the *Punjaub* and was a paddle steamer, but Willis converted it to a clipper sailing ship, and renamed it *Tweed*. From this ship, certain features were incorporated into the design of the *Cutty Sark*, which may be described as an improved *Tweed*.

Many accounts have been written about the clipper ships and their thrilling races to get back first with their cargoes to Britain, but the *Cutty Sark* was pre-eminent and is now the last and only link with the history of fast sailing ships and the Port of Berwick, and its mariners.

The Cutty Sark, as depicted in 1872 by artist Frederick Tudgay.

LAST ORDERS

It is likely that the smacks and their crews would be well regarded by Berwick's citizens, and one manifestation of this is the number of public houses and taverns with reference to smacks in their names.

So in 1806, we have Captain John Sample, named as the publican at the *"Sign of the Smack"* in Eastern Lane.

In Spittal at the same time was a public house named simply *"Smack"*, the tenant being Robert Thomson.

Today there is one tavern still existing which has a direct link with the Berwick Smacks and that is The Albion situated at the crossroads in Spittal. Listed on the departure and arrival board displayed on the London Wharf in 1812 was the smack *Albion*.

There was previously an Albion Inn in the Castlegate, Berwick, 1855.

c. 1891

In 1822 a tavern at Bridge End, Berwick, went by the title of *"Berwick Smack"*, the tenant being a Wm. Brown. While in Spittal there was again *"Smack"* – tenant Robert Wilson.

The *'London and Berwick'* smack gave its name to another hostelry situated in the Sandgate, as shown in a map of 1855, and the jug (illustrated) was no doubt presented to Mrs Douglass, the licensee of the London and Berwick Tavern in 1850, by appreciative patrons.

This picture of The Hen and Chickens Hotel shows an adjoining building, which was the gable end of The London & Berwick Tavern. Circa 1880.

A finely engraved ale goblet contemporary with the hey day of the Berwick Smack, circa 1822.

One Inn which existed in 1822 was the Ship Inn in Spittal, which was demolished in the 1930's. It was a clay built structure (i.e. built without mortar) and was photographed in the third quarter of the 19th century.

*Launch of the luxury yacht Audela in 1979.
It was completed in 1980 after which ship building ceased in Berwick.
The Audela is the ultimate in modern electro/mechanically
controlled sailing and has been widely featured on TV
and in the sailing world press.*

'Ceres' of Berwick. Circa 1797

This is Jim Walker's tenth
book on Berwick-upon-Tweed.
He has, over several decades
researched and documented the
town's history, its people, and its
Salmon Fishing Industry.

In this, his 95th year,
he completes his collection with
a fascinating insight into the ship
that was known as

The Berwick Smack

Previous titles by the author

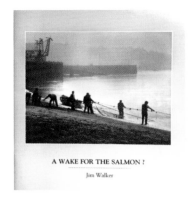

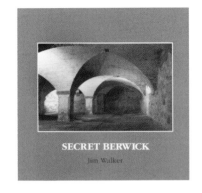

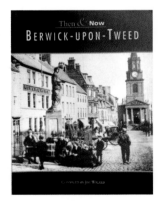

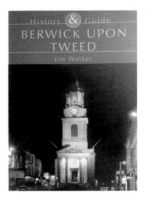

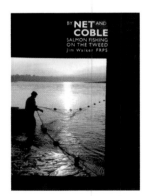

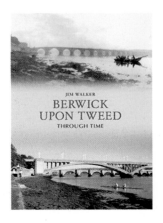

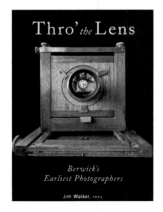